Acknowledgements

I'd like to thank all my friends and family members who supported me in my efforts in publishing my first book. I'd like to thank my daughter, Audrey Williams, for all her help and support. I'd also like to thank Armando Florencio, – graphic designer for my book cover design and website design page. mando@mandocentrik.com

Website=www. escapingvvrole.com
Facebook: Boundaries Work
Twitter @volunteervictim

Chapter 1 – Why some relationships fail

We are going to explore some of the reasons why some relationships are in good standing, why some relationships require far too much maintenance, why some have gone adrift, and why others have capsized and should be dissolved. The main ingredient that keeps a relationship from going adrift can be summed up in one word – RESPECT. We all know that it takes two people, along with their individualities as well as their ideologies, to have a successful relationship.

Looking for a mate who is somewhat compatible with your likes and dislikes can be a difficult task. However, it can be attainable. Keep one thing in mind: there is no perfect mate. And then again, would you really want a perfect mate? Coming relatively close to acquiring one should be considered a success in its own right. After all, maintaining a healthy and happy relationship in itself can prove to be quite challenging, although possible. What makes this process so challenging is the genetic disposition we all uniquely have. Some of us have our own philosophies about religion, raising children, politics, and science, just to name a few. These are what I like to refer to as individualities. Some of our individualities can also be referred to as idiosyncrasies. You know, those strange and peculiar habits, likes, and dislikes that we all have.

Hence the reason why when we are in pursuit of a relationship, we must take careful steps in learning about the behavior of the person we are seeking to make a commitment to. This can be done through a probationary period. Like in any platonic relationship, just by talking, interacting, and through time, you will be able to understand what an individual's position is on several fronts. I find that through conversation, people tend to disclose to you exactly what their position is on any issue that you bring up – via dialogue.

So through dialogue, you will be able to form an honest assessment of that individual. And this assessment will help you make a determination as to whether you want this person to play any role in your life. Oftentimes many of us jump in feet first and then attempt to perform the analysis afterwards. Nah, this not the correct course of action to take. In the long run, not being in such a hurry to get into a relationship will save you time and energy if you suddenly discover that you are unhappy. When a relationship ends, no party comes out of it unscathed. Or at least most of us don't.

If you go into a relationship head first, before you put in your feet, you stand a better chance of having a more peaceful and successful recovery should the relationship end. On the other hand, going into a relationship FEET first, when you try to escape from it, will prove to be far more difficult.

Sometimes in relationships we surrender our individualities without understanding that these features represent an integral part of who we are as a person. So when you commit to a relationship what the concentration should be on is combining both individualities to the point where they complement each other. And then just sit back and let TIME do what it does, TELL THE STORY.

The key ingredients for healthy relationships for the most part are established through what could be defined as a *learned* behavior. If the learned behavior is managed correctly, most relationships will be successful.

Of course, most relationships that you develop in your teenage years and perhaps your early twenties will be spent acquiring this learned behavior. No doubt during this time you will exhibit adolescent behavior in your relationships, and rightfully so, because you are still relatively new to the game. So after you have kissed a few frogs, you should be able to, in your later years, manage a relationship relatively stress-free – with the person you've chosen to make a solid commitment to.

When you ultimately decide to make a commitment to someone, you should have in place an established set of boundaries that will assist you in keeping your relationship healthy and strong. Boundaries in a relationship are simply limitations and restrictions that will assist you in your efforts in keeping, the relationship, for the most part, healthy and strong. You must have boundaries. They are absolutely essential in every relationship you encounter throughout your life. Establishing boundaries with respect to your significant other will insure that you *push back* in a relationship when you see it heading in the wrong direction.

These boundaries can and should be used in many different types of relationships: family / professional / intimate / friendship, to name but a few. You see, boundaries will prevent you from becoming a *victim* to someone else's circumstances. And having these set boundaries with respect to your mate will also enable your relationship to become quite blissful, providing that the person you have chosen to make the commitment to, respects your boundaries. These boundaries also act as a shield, or coat of armor. Without boundaries in every aspect of your life, you will ultimately *volunteer* to help continue someone else's bad behavioral habits. And once you continue to allow yourself to accept bad behavior from your significant other, you will have placed yourself in the precarious position of remaining in a failing or unhappy relationship that will ultimately fail. You might initially start out as a victim, but your continued acceptance of bad behavior is what will ultimately mold you into becoming a volunteer.

There are two roads that lead to every destination – the road that takes you *to* that destination and the road that takes you *away* from that destination. The instances that will be cited in this book are nothing more than circumstances that we face throughout our daily lives. I'm sure everybody has a story to tell. Typically, some men who constantly exhibit bad behavior are usually the ones that women have allowed to come into their lives through what in some instances can be referred to, as the back door. And this is where the problems will most certainly start to occur.

Once you have begun to recognize that your significant other doesn't feel that your needs are as valid as his, you should consider this to be a sign that the relationship may be in trouble. When you have acknowledged that you are constantly failing in your attempts to reconcile the issues within your relationship, this is a sure sign that the relationship will ultimately fail.

When you begin to accept the bad behavior of your significant other, this is also a definite sign that the relationship is heading downhill. When you start to feel that you are losing that assurance of love and start heading in the direction of bitterness, this is a sign that you are not in a relationship any longer, but instead you are in a "relationshit." When a relationship starts to deteriorate, you will begin to see the telltale signs. Your feelings will start to change for your significant other. You will begin to lose respect for your significant other. You will also begin to compromise your integrity.

You may also adapt the "I don't care anymore" attitude. It is at this time that you should begin to execute a plan for escaping. Staying in a failing or unhappy relationship can have damaging effects on you. Staying can become extremely stressful. When you begin to recognize that your emotional stability is being compromised, it becomes a matter of accepting the fact that you must move on, no matter how difficult it may seem. So now that you have begun to entertain thoughts of exiting out of your failing or unhappy relationship, it will be certain that you will be faced with obstacles.

The goal is to maneuver around whatever obstacles you encounter. You must also rid yourself of any and all apprehensions you will begin to encounter. This should help prepare you for getting ready for your departure – to even make a run for the border if necessary. If you ponder giving your significant other a stay of execution this will make it even more difficult to follow through with your plan of escaping. Once you have conquered these obstacles, you will be on your way to becoming equipped with the tools you will need to prepare for your dismount.

Victim or Volunteer? If you and your mate are constantly arguing over the same issues, that is putting a strain on your relationship, and in the end there is no resolution; the pattern will develop into a huge cloud that will hang over the relationship and keep it from going through its normal cycle of growth and development. When issues in a relationship go unresolved, this will keep it in constant friction. It is these types of differences that need to be addressed and remedied. Nobody should want a relationship that requires a tremendous amount of maintenance. Some issues within a relationship can be medicated; others you must remedy.

Chapter 2 – Tackling existing problems in your relationship

If there are problems within a relationship that are insurmountable, then this is indicative that the time has come to put the relationship down. Some storms within a relationship can be weathered, and then there are others that can't be. A method for tackling differences within a relationship can be to employ the triple A and E technique. The first A is to become AWARE of the issues that are putting a strain on the relationship. The second A is to ACCEPT that the issues do exist. The third and most important A is to take the ACTION needed to resolve the issue. Lastly is the E effect. And this is to ELIMINATE the issues that are causing friction within the relationship.

As an example of utilizing the AAAE effect, let's say you're two years into a relationship and your significant other has children by another woman and he has visitation privileges every other weekend. So now you know ahead of time what you are both going to be doing "every other weekend." But then all of a sudden the other woman starts intruding on the weekend that you and he spend alone with each other. You realize that this has become a pattern that has been going on for months and months.

First you address the issue with your significant other to let him know that this is causing a problem within the relationship. That's making him AWARE. Then you both accept and acknowledge that this is indeed creating a problem in your relationship. This means that you have now ACCEPTED what has to be done. Then he has to let his children's mother know that she needs to stick to the initial agreement of his having the kids every other weekend (not the weekend she chooses) and he has to stay firm in this conviction. This is the ACTION. Lastly now that it has been firmly established that the kids are coming every other weekend as prescribed (and this decision is adhered to), the problem has been ELIMINATED. Not knowing or practicing the techniques on how to resolve issues can put so much strain on a relationship that it becomes burdensome.

Mastering this requires the skills required to maintain a healthy relationship. If you at least make an attempt, your relationship has a chance of surviving. You must address issues that are causing stress in your relationship if you want it to prosper in a healthy way. In short, in relationships it is essential to be able to compromise and negotiate through the issues that are putting a strain on the relationship.

Some of us remain in relationships that are totally unhealthy for our well-being. And if there are children involved, it's certainly not healthy for them. And some of us make up excuse after excuse and try to rationalize and convince ourselves to stay in failing or unhappy relationships. If you remain in a such a relationship, it will eat at the core of your being. It will gnaw at the core of your very existence. It will become a slow pill of destruction. It'll make your morale low; you'll start to experience mood swings; the stress may become so unbearable that you could even end up with stress-related illnesses. You may develop ulcers. Your skin may break out. You may start to lose your hair. You may begin to lose weight. You may attempt to seek medication to help you cope with the stress. Your temper may become short with the kids. You may begin to feel that you are on the edge of a cliff.

Victim or Volunteer? We all make mistakes. We have all accepted bad behavior from our mates from time to time. However, when these bad behavioral practices keep constantly happening, you will have to come to the realization that it would be better for you to leave rather than stay. You have to know when it is time to move on. Don't begin to dwell on the time you have invested in this relationship. Electing to stay simply because of the time you have invested is one of the most common mistakes some of us make. Hanging on because you have invested time and energy won't make the relationship any better. In all probability it will become worse and more difficult for you to plan your exit strategy.

When you begin to realize that there is no method to your madness, you should start to consider your options. You will then begin to weigh the option of staying vs. leaving. When you have begun to realize that you are in a failing or unhappy relationship and you elect to stay, you are no longer a victim, you are a volunteer. As a volunteer, you begin to think that you are stuck and you don't see any way out. There are only three things that you can be stuck on. The first thing you can be stuck on is the LOVE; the second thing you can be stuck on is the SEX. The third thing you can be stuck on – as in most cases when people stay in failing or unhappy relationhips – is STUPIDITY.

Which one are you stuck on?

More often than not, some of us will begin to complain to our friends or family members about the problems in our relationship/relationshit. You may not expose to them all the explicit details out of fear of embarrassment, but nevertheless, each time you complain you're probably looking for some degree of sympathy.

Being realistic, how could you expect sympathy for a situation that you are allowing to continue? Are you really a victim, or are you a volunteer? Some people find it tremendously hard to get out of a failing or unhappy relationship. And then you have those strong-minded individuals who simply know when it's time to move on. Some individuals will ponder the thought of where they are going to move on to. Realize one thing: sometimes moving on to an unknown place could prove to be far better than staying in the predicament that you currently find yourself in. Sometimes you must learn how to get out of your own way. A great many of us fear the unknown. What you should fear, is what you know.

You have to ask yourself, is something better than nothing? Or is nothing better than a little something? Does the prospect of raising those kids all by yourself frighten you? Does the prospect of not having his money as a contribution to the household frighten you? Does the prospect of being alone frighten you? Some individuals do find these prospects frightening, and because of this, they compromise their integrity and elect to stay in a failing or unhappy relationship and continue to accept the bad behavior of their significant other.

There goes the excuse for staying when you know you should be going. You can't hold on and let go too! When you make the conscious decision to stay in a failing or unhappy relationship, know that you have just signed on for prolonged agony. By staying, also know that you have just volunteered to take on the bad behavior of your significant other longer that you should. So, in effect, truthfully, it is now is a bad habit that you have become accustomed to. As a result, everything bad that happens in the relationship from that point forward will not make you a victim – instead you will be a volunteer. You will be a volunteer that has deluded yourself into thinking that your failing or unhappy relationship might get better. This thinking simply amounts to nothing more than dragging out the ending, prolonging the inevitable.

Chapter 3 - Why some of us STAY in failing/unhappy relationships

Let's talk about some of the reasons people stay in failing or unhappy relationships/relationshit. Just because you have children together should not be used as an excuse to allow someone to manipulate you in any way with their bad behavior. Some of us will even offer a reason/excuse that they want their children to know who their father/mother is. Just because the significant other is out of your life doesn't mean that he/she can't play the parent role in the lives of the children. Or does it? Some individuals will use their children as pawns in an attempt to keep the relationship going.

If you are in a relationship that is full of anger and resentment, it can have an irreversible and detrimental effect on the children if you elect to stay. There are certain environments to which children should not be exposed, especially if there are physical confrontations. Do you want your children to constantly witness Daddy physically abusing Mommy, or vice versa? When children constantly witness physical confrontations between adults, there is a greater chance that the children will begin to think that this is normal behavior. Remember, children tend to emulate what they see. Just because you still LOVE your significant other should not be used as an excuse to stay in a failing or unhappy relationship. If you elect to stay in a failing or unhappy relationship because you LOVE him/her, you are not a victim, you are a volunteer. Have you ever loved and hated someone at the same time? There is really no such thing as a love/hate relationship.

What is described as a love/hate relationship really boils down to the fact that you may LOVE the person you are with, but it's things that the person does or says that release the emotion of HATE.

Sometimes through force, we need to leave a person that we love in order to keep our own peace of mind. You see, leaving a failing or unhappy relationship will give you the opportunity to re-group and re-evaluate yourself to the extent that you concentrate on conditioning yourself into becoming a better and stronger person who has learned from past mistakes. It's ironic, but some people learn quicker and become better through failure of all kinds.

Sometimes you can love a person to the point where it becomes dangerous and you've got to leave them. Some people love too deeply. Too deeply to the extent where they will allow their significant other to wreak havoc upon them and in the process, they lose their self-respect. Sometimes you have to weigh the feeling of love you have for that person against your sanity and then decide which one is more important to you and the fiber of your being.

You should always love yourself more than you love your significant other. You should never lose your individuality, not even in a unit such as marriage. If your relationship is not right in your head, how could it be right in your heart? If you remain in a failing or unhappy relationship, it could be because of that deep emotion of love that ultimately convinces you to accept and do things that ordinarily you would not do.

The love you have for a person may also make you accept bad behavior from that person indefinitely. It can induce you into doing things that take you outside of what should be considered normal behavior. Things such as searching his/her cell phone, searching pockets. When you begin to stoop to the point where you are checking cell phone correspondence, searching pockets, I certainly hope that you have prepared yourself for what you may find.

You may even begin to question the whereabouts of your significant other – following him/her, calling phone numbers you may find (via snooping) in a cell phone. And these are just to name a few. I think you get the picture.

The prospect of being alone frightens some of us to the extent that we will remain in failing or unhappy relationships. And when we do, we are no longer victims – we are volunteers. And when you volunteer, be prepared to suffer heartbreak after heartbreak. All individuals should learn how to spend time by themselves. It gives you a chance to explore your inner being and to become in touch with who you really are and what you really want for yourself. You must learn to love yourself more than you love the person you are in the relationship with.

By moving into an uncommitted state, perhaps you can attempt to replenish some of that self-esteem you surrendered while you were in your failing or unhappy relationship. Find other things to focus on. Try to regain the confidence you may have once had in yourself. Try to remember how important you should be to yourself. Try to remember that you don't deserve to be in a failing or unhappy relationship. Take all that energy you exerted in trying to keep a failing or unhappy relationship together that should have ended a long time ago, and invest in something more positive – like your children, yourself, your family. In short, venture into something more worthwhile, something that's going to lift you up, not tear you down.

Take the time to set boundaries for your next relationship. We should all have boundaries in our relationships, boundaries that won't allow you to end up in the same predicament you are attempting to escape from right now. Having no boundaries can be a reason that many people remain in failing or unhappy relationships. On the other hand, having boundaries will help you to better navigate through and out of, a bad situation. The boundaries will become forbidden territories for someone who exhibits bad behavior, should he try to become an object of your affection. These forbidden territories, if invaded, will make you surrender your integrity and accept the bad behavior of people who can cause you to move out of your COMFORT ZONE. Having boundaries acts as a cushion which will enable you to remain within your comfort zone which equals being STRESS FREE... or at the very least, minimally stressed!

Let's explore the options of having boundaries vs. NOT having boundaries in a relationship. Keep in mind that boundaries are nothing more than principles which you live by. For example, if you are in the dating arena you will already know ahead of time what you simply will NOT tolerate if a man comes at you with GAME. By having your defined set of boundaries, you will be able to turn that engine OFF quickly. So when and if someone approaches you with that GAME mentality, right away you will say "NAW, it's not going down like that. C YAH! And DON'T holler back!"

Setting boundaries enables you to put your course(s) of action in place in the event that the relationship takes a turn for the worse. This way you know ahead of time what you would do in the event that you find out that your significant other has cheated. You will know ahead of time what course of action you will take in the event your significant other gives you an STD. You will also know ahead of time what course of action you will take if you catch him cheating. You will also know what course of action you will take if you catch him constantly lying about his whereabouts. You will also know what course of action you will take if a baby by another woman is conceived outside of the relationship. These are just to name a few. Having these boundaries will make what might be a hard decision for someone who has NO boundaries, easier for you, simply because you have boundaries.

If you are in a relationship and you have NO boundaries, you become automatically conditioned to becoming a volunteer. If you have boundaries, you are automatically conditioned to NOT becoming a victim for an extended period of time. You must have morals and principles that you live by. It's as simple as that.

A lot of women have allowed and accepted bad behavior from their significant other. Bad behavior that should NOT be tolerated whatsoever. Examples of bad behavior include a constant cheater, a constant batterer, someone who gives you a STD, or someone who produced a baby while you were in a relationship with him. Why would you want to remain in a relationshit when you have been violated in this respect?

Yeah I know: you're staying because you love him. Have we become *that* desperate? For some of us the answer is yes, and the answer is yes because some of us are just that desperate. And it's out of desperation that you have allowed yourself to continue to volunteer for the nonsense, the bad behavior of your significant other. And that's exactly what you will continue to volunteer for – nonsense. A lot of women have allowed men to simply wreak havoc upon them. Some people are of the opinion that- women should "act like a lady and think like a man." You don't need to think like a man. All you need to do is THINK period.

You don't need to attempt to perform an analysis on how you believe a man will think or act in any given situation. Just analyze how YOU would think/respond in unexpected situations that may come your way. You are not a man, so why would you need to THINK like one? I understand the concept of trying to predict how a man would react in any given situation. However, the concentration should NOT be on what you predict his reaction might be. Instead it should be on exactly what his action was.

In other words, you can't try to predict where a moving target might land. So many women have allowed men to make volunteers out of them. The men who exhibit bad behavior constantly do so, because women are signing off on their bad behavior by their continued acceptance of it. As the saying goes, if you don't stand for something, you will fall for anything. You'll fall for all the lies that they tell you. You'll fall for the games they play with you. You'll fall for the empty promises they make to you.

A lot of women have fallen for the trap some men have set for them. Some women have fallen for anything, and in the process they have lost their moral integrity. When you lose your moral integrity, you are no longer able to compute how this situation will affect you in the long run. Some women have no shame whatsoever. You should NEVER compromise your integrity for the sake of being in a relationship / relationshit! When you compromise your integrity, everything that was sacred to you goes out the window. In short, you have relinquished any stronghold you may have had. You no longer have any muscle to flex. And I'm certainly NOT talking about the muscle between your legs.

Chapter 4 – **You do NOT have to accept bad behavior**

Lots of women constantly accept bad behavior from their significant other. Some women have accepted bad behavior for so long that they are to the point where they have convinced themselves that this is normal behavior. Some women have deluded themselves into thinking that the majority of men behave in this manner. Some women have simply allowed themselves to be preyed upon. One incident of infidelity can perhaps be forgiven. However, if you have evidence of your man cheating, not just once or twice but several times, why would you want to continue to be with that man? Why would you want to continue the relationship, knowing what you know?

When you continue to have sex with a man once you have confirmation of his cheating, you are setting yourself up to play the role of the volunteer. And when you accept the role of a volunteer, you have given him permission to continue with this bad behavior. When men exhibit bad behavior, that bad behavior should be met with consequences. And the consequences should be harsh enough for them to think long and hard before they put the relationship at risk again. And when I say consequences, I don't mean that they should be placed in a corner for a time out. They need to be made aware of the fact that should they continue with their bad behavior, the repercussions will be so severe that they may lose you and the relationship. You certainly don't reward them by having another baby by them. Now if the relationship is NOT important to them, they will continue with the bad behavior. On the other hand, if the relationship IS important to them, they'll know exactly how they should behave if their primary objective is to KEEP the relationship. It's as simple as that.

If you have experienced any of the above, and if you elect to stay in that relationship and continue to engage in sex with that man, you must realize that you have just signed on to receive the slow doses of poison that he will continue to feed you while you remain in that failing or unhappy relationship. When you continue to engage in sexual activity with your mate after he has constantly exhibited bad behavior, what you are in effect doing is rewarding him.

And when you keep constantly rewarding him for the bad behavior, you'll get to the point where you won't even be able to recognize yourself anymore. Keep one thing in mind: you can no longer claim that you are a victim of circumstances. Instead you are now indeed a volunteer – period! If you continue to accept this bad behavior from him, not only are you a volunteer; you also own it! YUP! You just purchased and paid for it in full.

And while you continue to suck up the poison, eventually you'll get to the point within the relationship where it becomes even more difficult for you to recover should you decide to leave. What many women don't understand is that men will continue to exhibit bad behavior as long as they give them permission to do so. This is where the boundaries take effect. Without boundaries, you risk becoming a volunteer. If you have boundaries, you stand a better chance of NOT becoming a victim.

Some women have NO standards at all with respect to men. Most women will continue to go through the revolving door of men who exhibit bad behavior. That revolving door is, in effect, their permission slip administered by you. Some women have convinced themselves that this is what men will do, and that all men exhibit this type of behavior. This is not true. All men DO NOT behave in this manner. Men who exhibit bad behavior do so because women allow them to. Yes, it's just that simple. Remember the old saying – *Can't ANYBODY take advantage of you without your permission*. This is a true statement.

A lot of women find it easier to place the blame on the man. Being realistic, sometime we as women must take ownership of staying with a man who exhibits this type of bad behavior. Women that choose to stay in failing or unhappy relationships sometimes do so out of desperation. They also do so because they have low self-esteem. Women who have no moral integrity will remain in a failing or unhappy relationship *just because*. And when women stay in a failing or unhappy relationship, oftentimes unbeknownst to them, they have just bought a lifetime membership to the NOT for PROFIT organization of women who stay in failing or unhappy relationships.

Some women need to take a long, hard look into the mirror, and in doing so, some will discover fault within themselves. If you are the type who frequents the clubs in outfits that reveal far more than they should, who dresses in a manner that doesn't leave much to the imagination, to a man that speaks volumes about your character. Or worse yet, if you sleep with a man after you have only known him for one day or a couple of days, a month or so, that too speaks volumes about your character. Why would you risk sleeping with a man at that early stage in the game before you have explored his past sexual behavior? Especially in this day and age, we should take our time to seek all the information required before we place ourselves at risk sexually.

When you appear to be easy, you're going to be labeled "easy." Most men look for the many things that attract them to women. And some of these attractions are short term. Women should be very careful in the way that they express themselves sexually to a man before finding out if there will be longevity to the relationship, providing that longevity is what you are seeking. Constantly wearing low cut blouses, or parading yourself around in clubs looking for men to buy you drinks does not set a good example of who you are as a woman.

Some men only seek out women who are looked upon as being EASY. And if you present the EASY picture of yourself to him, what you are in effect letting him know is that you are vulnerable, and that for him the HUNT is on. If he sees that it is easy for him to get into your panties, he will also know that it is easy for any other man to get into your panties as well. That's the mini bio of yourself that you have just given to him.

When you have NOT put forth any boundaries or standards with respect to yourself -that becomes self-evident to a man. He will know just how much energy he'll need to exert in order for him to establish whatever role in your life he chooses to play. There are lots of men who want women who are easy. That's because they know that not much effort will be required to obtain exactly what it is that he wants. And if sex is primarily what he is seeking, he will know that not much is required of him in terms of courtship. He knows that he is not faced with too much of a challenge in winning you over, so to speak. If men are made to feel that there are no guidelines for them to follow and that the bar is set very low, they immediately know that their pursuit of you will not be that difficult.

In some instances you will meet men who simply DO NOT KNOW how to pursue a woman they claim to be interested in. If a man is truly interested in a woman, his art of pursuit should be very intriguing and profound. If a man executes the pursuit, it is at this juncture that he knows exactly what role he wants to play in your life.

If a man has not set a course of pursuit towards a woman he claims to be interested in, then you must ask yourself, what is it that he is really looking for? Is he looking for a jump off? If SEX is his only interest in you, then he knows that his task will be a simple one. He will know that there is only one area which requires his total concentration, and that will be getting you into his bed – nothing more, nothing less. When you make it easy for a man to have sex with you, 90% of his pursuit and courtship is over.

You must put mechanisms in place for him that will ensure that SEX is at the very back of the courtship list. Women must learn to be able, by way of boundaries and standards, to ward off a man who is simply seeking sexual gratification. Having boundaries will help you to determine when and if you think the time is right to engage in a sexual encounter with a potential mate. During the dating process, it is you who should determine when the appropriate time is for both of you to engage in your first sexual encounter. You shouldn't give up the sex boundary too early. To do so, takes away any leverage you may have relative to seeking longevity in a possible relationship.

Until the time comes when you begin to feel comfortable to engage in the first sexual encounter with a potential mate, know that you can sleep alongside a man and NOT engage in a sexual relationship with him. If you are dating or being courted by a man, and let's say it's only been two months, you can sleep alongside him and NOT have sex with him. And it is very important for you to be able to experience this act. That means you are in control. It means that you have NOT relinquished your standards or principles at the beginning of this relatively new relationship.

You would be able to process it a lot better if you did NOT give up the sex boundary during this probationary period, if he decided that he no longer wanted to date you. However, on the other hand if you had given up the SEX too early during the probationary period and he decided that he no longer wanted to date you, then just imagine how this would make you feel. Your ego would be bruised if you didn't get the call back that you were looking for and hoping to receive.

The probationary period affords you the opportunity to see if this person is consistent in his behavior. Does he call when he says he will? Does he the meet you at the scheduled time? Do you see him every weekend or every other weekend? Do you see him during the holidays? If you pay close attention to his behavior during the probationary period, you'll be able to gather the data you need to determine if you want to continue the process that may eventually lead you to having this person in your life for an extended period of time.

Having boundaries/standards affords you the opportunity to see exactly what type of man it is that you are dealing with. Having this knowledge allows you to make an educated and informed decision in terms of whether you will want to continue with this. You know exactly what type of person he really is. Remember now, in the beginning of the relationship prospect, or not. However, if you give up the *cookie* too early, you have no one to blame but yourself.

Don't be afraid to set boundaries/standards (if you don't already have some in place) while in the probationary period of a relatively new relationship. If he's interested, he'll stick around and wait until you feel comfortable commencing with the sexual aspect of the relationship. If he's not that interested in you, rest assured, he will most definitely bounce. Also while you are still in the preliminary stages of the courtship, be sure to keep your eyes and ears wide open. By keeping your eyes and ears open, you will be able to see so many important things about him that will tell the REAL story about his intentions relative to you.

During the probationary period, you should be able to see at this juncture, what type of man he really is. It's at this juncture that he tells you HIS story. He will reveal things to pursue you, he's quite polished. However as time goes by, if you're listening one of two things will happen: Either he will remain polished, or his coat of paint will start to peel.

Make sure you are paying very close attention. If you are paying close attention, this should help you to decide which pile he may ultimately be placed on. As a single person in the dating arena, you will have 1 to 3 of what I refer to as "piles." He might go into the #1 "Let's-just-be-friends" pile, or #2 the "Loser" pile, or # 3, the "Potential" pile.

Truth be told, you DON'T really want a "Let's-just-be-friends" pile. If you know that he's a loser, feel free and confident as you place him in the "Loser" pile. And just keep moving on to the next one! Set boundaries and standards. Once you have set them, DON'T FORGET THEM. Don't think like a man, but do act like a lady. Remember, those who have no boundaries are rendered powerless. While on the other hand, those who have boundaries are rendered powerful. You have to bring your boundary game to the table as well. Don't just sit back and allow him to bring his! Let him know what you are working with! Intertwine them, and let the chips fall where they may.

If you are in your late 30s or beyond, by this time in your life you have probably experienced a few relationships. And if you're single and in your 30s or beyond, you should definitely know by now how to spot a Loser from quite a far distance. You will know how to spot him because of the boundaries and standards that you not only live by, but have also incorporated into your life. I can't emphasize enough why having boundaries will enable you to process a multitude of life's experiences differently. It's a tool you've got to have in your arsenal. You're pretty much done without it. Without boundaries you may constantly find yourself in that volunteer role. And if you have any degree of intellect, you'll know that's not the role you want to play. So don't even sign up for it.

Chapter 5 – Heartache, pain and stress that you can avoid

Do you know what's frightening about this whole concept of women who remain in failing or unhappy relationships?

They go on to have daughters and have absolutely NO morals, values or principles to teach them and thus, the saga continues. It can become a ripple effect for years to come. If you don't have good morals and values to pass along to your children, then what could you possibly expect them to pass on to *their* children? The boundaries that you set forth should without question, be taught to your daughters.

Why? Because sometimes young women allow young boys to whisper sweet nothings in their ears, and when they do so, some of these young women will take what they say literally. And the young women will fall for the okie-dokie. These young women should be taught that just because a young man tells you that he loves doesn't necessarily mean that he does. While they are in the preliminary stages of a relationship they are seeking, let them know that they must pay close attention to his actions.

You see some of these young women who have not been taught to look for morals and values in a young man, make the mistake of taking a young man at his word and end up in a predicament they aren't prepared to handle. An example of a predicament they are unable to handle is giving birth to a child long before they have had the opportunity to experience life in any meaningful aspect. Some of these young women end up have baby after baby. Some go on to have many babies as though they are accessories. And some do so without knowing that the relationship can be over before they baby is even born. And they do so because no one taught them how important it is to "just say no." No one taught them how important it is to have boundaries. Mentally, most of these young girls are babies themselves. So what could they possibly teach their children?

I can't stress the importance of teaching your daughters, especially, that having a baby or babies at a very young age can lead them on toward a life of complete misery and hardship. Here's a picture that you can see becoming a reality for the many young women who haven't been taught some of the perils in life they can be faced with, should they decide to embark on a road to nothingness. It might play out something like this. #1 Girl plans on attending college after graduating from high school. #2 Boy meets girl. #3 Boy woos girl (whispering sweet nothings in her ear) and girl becomes pregnant. #4 Girl decides to have baby and she's, let's say, she's 17-19. #5 Girl delivers baby and now looks to support child. # 4 Boy is gone, because he had no idea what the responsibility of what raising a child would entail. #6 Girl is forced to drop out of school to raise child alone. #7 Girl and boy continue to talk off and on because now they truly have something in common – a BABY. #8 Girl forced to drop out of school, college is put on hold, time passes by and oops, here comes another baby…The point is that having children at a very young age GREATLY diminishes any aspirations you may have had of finishing high school, or going to college.

Now their life has taken a turn onto a journey they are totally NOT prepared for. This is NOT a good place to START FROM on your journey through life.
It is your responsibility to teach them not to be so gullible to things people promise them, especially promises made by boys in the name of love. Teach them that just because a boy professes his love for them, does not mean that he truly loves you. Let them know that he may only be telling you that because his primary focus is to get inside your panties. Let your daughters know that all this attention he is paying to them now could disappear as soon as they decide to have sex with each other. Let your girls know that if they make the decision to engage in sex at an early age, they must do so responsibly.   Let them know also that the repercussions of not acting responsibly can result in STDs, emotional turmoil, unwanted pregnancies and abortions. Let them know the importance of not trying to win a popularity contest by engaging in sex

because that seems to be what everybody else is doing.

If these young girls had any aspiration to go to college, they must be made aware that having a baby too early in life will greatly diminish any chance of this, or even of finishing high school for that matter. You must teach them how important it is to explore the potential of that young man in whom they currently have an interest. Make them understand the importance of knowing and exploring a potential relationship with a young man before they delve in too deeply. You must teach them how to initiate the exploration process. Explain to them what it is that they should be looking for in a young man.

They need to be taught how to explore his potential for finishing school, his potential with respect to going to college, his potential for becoming a responsible person, his potential for becoming a productive member of society. You should teach them how to explore whether he would be willing to work in McDonald's as opposed to striving to become a drug dealer because he thinks it's fast money. In short, teach them what to look for so they will know what direction he is headed for in life. Learned lessons ensure that you don't repeat past mistakes. But if you, as a woman, are the Volunteer type, there isn't much you will be able to teach your daughters. Teaching the positive aspects of learned behavior is essential in that it plays a significant role in the growth and development process of our children's lives.

It's very important that we teach our children the necessary learned behavior integral to their everyday lives in order for them to have some degree of happiness in a relationship or success in their lives.

Some parents today simply don't take the time to teach their children to have morals, values, or principles. Things are not the way they used to be 30 or 40 years ago. When we make a decision to bring children into the world, it is no longer about us for the most part. Our attention has to gear toward helping our children to accomplish positive goals and aspirations in life. There are a lot of things that we as parents will need to sacrifice in order to raise our children to become productive members of society. There are sacrifices that all parents must make, because if you don't strive for your children to become the very best that they can be, they could possibly end up being lost in the world.

Take the energy you exert in trying to hold onto a failing or unhappy relationship and apply it towards your children to ensure that, at the very least, they are equipped to handle any relationship curve balls that may be thrown their way.

When we don't make the necessary investment in our children's growth and development process, more often than not, we have indirectly put them on a path of *nothingness*. And the path of nothingness includes following whatever trends are currently out there, including the trends of accepting bad behavior that you yourself, could have possibly introduced them to. As we all know, there are so many negative trends that our children can succumb to.

Some of these negative trends include getting "tramp stamps" otherwise known as tattoos. Oftentimes these tattoos are placed on the body where they are visible to almost everyone. Sometimes we make decisions in our younger years that follow us through, and affect us negatively, when we reach our adult life. For example, when you are 18 or 19 years old and you make a decision to get a tattoo of whatever, alongside side of your neck, when you attempt to seek employment somewhere in Corporate America, it would be naïve to expect an interviewer to take you seriously when you have a tattoo on your neck.

Another trend is wearing pants to the point that they are hanging off your butt. Another trend is not going to school so you can hang out with the other kids you know who don't go to school either. Another trend is constantly smoking "weed." Another is hanging out on the street corners with no positive destination in life, or drinking and smoking weed all day, and then sleeping the next day until late in the afternoon – or all day for that matter. These trends stem from kids thinking that they can do whatever they like because no one has put any *disciplines or boundaries* in place, and demanded that they adhere to them.

You must encourage your children to set goals for themselves. You must assist them in achieving these goals. It is your responsibility to equip them with the necessary tools that are required to ensure – or at least hope – that they achieve these goals and don't become *volunteers*.

Attempting to discipline or set boundaries for your children doesn't start when they become teenagers and begin to run amok. All children require a set of rules they must follow. When you raise a child without discipline or boundaries, further down the road that child could become a burden to you. You must set rules for your children to adhere to so that you don't volunteer for a lot of headaches and heartaches going forward, and also so that you don't become an enabler to the negative behavior they will exhibit when there are no boundaries in place.

As a parent, you must devote the necessary time to these children, because the world is a very tough place to live in day to day. You must prepare your children to face the reality of what life could possibly have in store for them, whether it is good, bad or indifferent.

There are a lot of negative forces out there that they could succumb to: gangs, prison, drugs, etc. As a parent, you bear the responsibility of trying to direct them away from those negative forces. And you must be smart in your attempts to do so by introducing them to *boundaries*. Let them know exactly what the repercussions could be, should they deviate from those set boundaries. And when you explain it to them, please – keep it real.

Chapter 6 – Boundaries and why they play an integral role in all relationships

Boundaries are the most important tool that you must have in your arsenal. If you have gotten out of a failing or unhappy relationship, this tool will greatly assist you into not falling in that trap again. You will be able to spot a LOSER more than a mile away. You must have your eyes open. Having your eyes open will enable you to have a general idea of a possible pattern of a man who may exhibit bad behavior. Boundaries will prevent you from going in feet first. This tool will ensure that you proceed with the utmost caution. Having boundaries will prevent you from allowing your expectations to be violated. There are several *strong women* who have taken the position in life that they would prefer being alone rather than allow a man to wreak havoc upon them. And what led them to this decision is quite simple: they have boundaries that are very well in place.

Boundaries teach women to neither accept nor entertain men whom they see exhibit bad behavior. Women with boundaries steer clear of men still trying to be a player. Women with boundaries are like the ones described in Raheem Devaugh's song titled "Woman." It's a great song that speaks about women that have boundaries. Not to mention it has a FUNKY beat!

Being properly equipped with boundaries enables you to make better decisions. Having boundaries essentially can be looked upon as having *official lines* you don't allow anyone to cross. An example of official lines that should not be crossed would be
1. If you came home and found your significant other in bed with someone else. 2. If you found your significant other abusing your children. 3. If you found out that your significant other had fathered a child outside of your relationship. Just to name a few. The official line limits and restricts your acceptance of behavior that should be deemed intolerable. If any of these official lines are crossed, the relationship should be DONE. End of story. That's a WRAP!

Having boundaries will prevent you from being miserable in a relationship. Boundaries will also help prevent you from going off the deep end. Boundaries will also prevent you from having a nervous breakdown. Boundaries will prevent you from allowing someone to take you completely outside of your character. Boundaries will enable you to reassure yourself that any bad situation can be made better. Boundaries will also enable you to run a bad situation through you thought process and come up with a viable solution that will keep your emotional well-being intact.

Boundaries will enable you to apply the correct formula for dealing with conflict. Boundaries will also prevent you from handing out free passes to

men who constantly exhibit bad behavior. Boundaries will prevent you from becoming overly stressed out. Boundaries will keep you on the right path to overcome any obstacles you may face.
Boundaries will make it easier for you to dismiss someone or something that is wearing you down.

Boundaries will keep you afloat in situations where, if you had no boundaries, in all probability, you would head into the abyss. Having boundaries will also prevent you from allowing yourself to become psychologically manipulated by anyone. Having boundaries will keep you from abandoning your inner most principles. Having boundaries will also prevent you from allowing the scars of love to turn into open wounds that you need to nurse for an extended period of time.

And ultimately, boundaries will prevent you from becoming a volunteer for misery. When you head into a relationship without any boundaries, you could be opening yourself up for lots of heartache and pain. Many women don't realize the power they possess in their relationship. And I'm not talking about the power between your legs. The power to set the wheels in motion and convince your significant other that bad behavior simply will NOT be accepted. There has to be a line drawn when it comes to accepting bad behavior. Without the line, the volunteer process begins. You must introduce yourself to the word NO.

You must also exercise the use of this word when required. And when you say the word NO, it must be said emphatically. This stuff is NOT rocket science. Men will constantly exhibit bad behavior when you continuously allow them to do so. The training process does not begin by attempting to teach them how to roll over, or how to go and fetch. The training process is nothing more than letting him know what will NOT be tolerated. The process begins when you explain to him that he doesn't have *carte blanche* to treat you like an inanimate object; nor to treat you without any respect. Most importantly, at the starting point of the relationship you must be abundantly clear in making him understand that the length of this relationship is contingent upon how he behaves and how serious HE wants this relationship to be – period. This is all providing that he agrees to make the commitment.

So now that you have laid the foundation for prosperity and peace within this relationship, the onus will be not just on him to keep the relationship healthy and strong; the onus is on you as well to keep up your end of the bargain. That means ensuring that you are doing your part as a woman to keep your significant other interested in keeping the relationship healthy.

Remember, good men expect to get from you the essentials they need in order to make them feel that the things they do for you are appreciated. It's not a one-way street. You as a woman have obligations to meet in satisfying your man, in order to make him think twice about going astray. You must make him feel that he is playing the lead role in the relationship. Then just sit back and let time do what it does: tell the story.

You must demand respect. If the time comes where you feel he is not living up to the standards that you have set in terms of keeping the relationship healthy and strong, it's time to analyze the direction the relationship is heading. Here is where you begin the process of deciding whether the relationship is worth holding onto, or whether it's time for you to sever the ties with him. If you elect to keep him while he continues to exhibit bad behavior, then rest assured you will be going through his revolving door of misery.

Just imagine the benefits if even just 75% of women practiced this methodology of having boundaries and enforcing them when it comes to relationships with the men they elect to play a significant role in their lives. Women who have boundaries will easily pull the trigger on men who exhibit bad behavior by dismissing them immediately. They know automatically what the possible outcome would be if they continue to seek a relationship with this type of man. I'm sure many of you think you know exactly when a relationship is truly defined as being "OVER."

For those of you, who don't, let me tell you. It's not over when you take the keys to the apartment/house away from him. It's not over when you stop cooking for him. It's not over when you stop doing his laundry. It's not over when you don't take his phone calls for a week or more. It's officially OVER when you STOP having SEX with him. That's when the relationship is really over. You see, often times when couples are going through what I call "relationshit" and one of them is upset with the other, they tend to go on what I call a STRIKE for a short period of time.

STRIKES while continuing to have SEX- simply means that you have placed a Band-Aid on the situation. Eventually, the Band-Aid will come off. And this means that you have reverted back to where you initially were in the relationship. With the continuation of SEX, even if you have said that it's over, you are simply postponing the inevitable. So in short, the saga continues. And the relationship will end up right back to square one again.

This is where the boundaries come in to play. Having these will better enable you to get through the nonsense behavior that you know in your heart of hearts, is not right. Having the boundaries will also make it easier for you to process the situation in your head when you contemplate exiting a failing or unhappy relationship.

Ultimately, having boundaries removes you from being stuck on stupid for an indefinite period of time. Having boundaries equips you with tools that you will need to prevent you from abandoning your principles. Having established boundaries will prevent you from bluffing. Without boundaries you may attempt to bluff your way out of bad behavior situations that you experience within your relationship. And that's all they will amount to – bluffs. And without these boundaries, in all probability, you will continue to volunteer. However, when you have such boundaries in place, they will supersede any acts of bluffing.

Chapter 7 – <u>Why standards are important</u>

Standards are important in that if you don't place any values on yourself or on your road to happiness, how will you be able to determine how you have fared thus far?

The standard of having developed your own financial independence and of having maintained the roof over your head is something to be very proud of. If you have also at the age of, let's say 25, completed four years of college and acquired a degree, this is something else to be proud of. And if, after these accomplished goals, you have made the decision to put off having children because you're still on the road to acquiring the stature that will place you in a position to be self-sustaining, that too, is a major achievement. If you've also landed a job and are now a professional in corporate America, this too, is a major achievement.

In short, you have managed and conditioned yourself to be able to stand on your own two feet. You must have principles that you follow throughout your journey in life. You must have the moral integrity NOT to allow someone to mistreat you for their gain. Your standards will prevent you from accepting the bad behavior of others. Your standards are the things in which you truly believe, and which will be very beneficial toward any endeavors you choose to undertake throughout your life. These standards that you have achieved will govern how you behave, and more importantly, how you allow others to behave toward you. Standards are nothing more than levels of quality that you use as a guide in situations that you encounter, levels of material comfort. They keep you in a comfort zone where you won't allow people to wreak havoc upon you personally or professionally.

Setting standards helps you to make better decisions in life.

Standards are the levels you want and expect for yourself. And setting these standards insures that the criteria you expect are met. They will only be met if you stand firm. These standards will shield you against the uncharacteristic behavior of others. One should never abandon their principles. If you have standards and are faced with something you have never encountered before, you won't place yourself in a position where you find yourself staring down the edge of a cliff wondering how you got there. Having standards will position you to be able to re-group and rebound from any unscrupulous acts brought upon you by someone else.

When you continuously accept the bad behavior of men, you are making it hard for the women who have boundaries, standards, principles. When a man who exhibits bad behavior encounters a woman with boundaries, standards and principles, he automatically thinks that if she doesn't go along with his nonsense, she has a problem. And why does he think this? He thinks this because of the many women he's dealt with in his past who allowed him to... what? Exhibit bad behavior!

Having standards, this coat of armor will help you navigate through life and any tough roads you may find yourself up against. And more importantly, you must remember that the standards that you elect to follow throughout your life, must not be set so high that you fall short of them when assessing what a potential mate is expected to bring to the table. In other words, don't have unrealistic standards. You shouldn't ask or expect a certain type of behavior from a potential mate that you yourself do not exhibit. By having unrealistic expectations, you may find yourself without a man for an extended period of time.

In short, if you have expectations or a certain set of criteria that a potential mate is supposed to meet, then you yourself should meet those very same criteria in a relationship where there may be a commitment to each other. If you are 5'5" and 200 lbs., have five kids and three different daddies, you should not be looking for a man who is 6', 150 lbs., with no kids. Come on now. Keep it real!

If you are a female who is sitting at home and who has been receiving public assistance for an extended period of time, it is truly unrealistic to set your sights on a man who is working a 9-5, and who lives alone in his own condo with no children and who may travel frequently. What else do you have to bring to the table, except sex, that will intrigue him to want to pursue anything via a permanent relationship with you?

This goes to the point that a man knows ahead of time what role he will assign you to play in his life. The only way you get to make that decision before him is if you have a set of boundaries in place that you insist that he abide by. However, if you expose your hand and that hand does not contain anything that a decent man would want to grasp, your hand is virtually empty. The point is, you are, in all probability, only going to get from that man something similar to what you have to offer him. And this is keeping it real.

Chapter 8 – **Respect for yourself and its benefits**

Respect yourself, and you will automatically command that others respect you as well. Without self-respect, you really can't expect anyone else to show you respect. When someone shows you respect, that means you have earned it. If you are the type of woman who goes to the club scantily dressed, you will be perceived by men in a negative way. When you constantly put your body on display, this will be the first thing a man sees about you. He will automatically see you as a possible easy lay.

When you go about – whether it's to a club or street fair – prancing around half-naked, that in itself speaks volumes about your character. When you exhibit this type of behavior, in all probability, you do so because you think you look sexy. You should know that many men define SEXY in several different ways. Trust me; you can look very sexy without revealing or exposing your breast, your butt, or your thong.

You must demand respect from all persons who are a part of your life. First and foremost, you must respect yourself. And having that respect will prevent people from playing games with you because they know you will not allow it. Having respect for yourself is not allowing some else to disrespect you.

We live in a world where a lot of people do not command respect. Some of us allow people in our lives to do and say anything to us without any repercussions. For example, if you meet a guy, after having several encounters with him – lunch, dinner, and movie – you should be able to tell if he is in some type of relationship with another woman. You should be able to tell if he is married, living with, or still messing with, his baby mama. He, in all probability, won't tell this to you.

And if you make the discovery that he is still involved with someone else, it is at this point in time where you should remove yourself from the equation. You must respect other people's relationships in the very same way that you want your relationship to be respected. Learning how to step away from a man who is somehow involved with another woman,-will prevent you from becoming a volunteer. If you choose to continue to indulge, you can only blame yourself for any gloom and doom you encounter with him going forward.

<u>Strength</u>
Having strength doesn't only mean being physically able to endure life's possible hardships. Having strength means being adaptable. Having strength means being financially able to maintain your household on your own in the event that you decide that the relationship you are holding onto must be dissolved. Having strength means being able to

withstand any difficulties you may all of a sudden find yourself faced with. Having strength means having the wherewithal to keep your ship from sinking. Having strength means being able to reposition yourself, should you be faced with one of life's many perils. Having boundaries in place will no doubt enable your strength to kick in before you get to the point where you may think that you are stuck.

When you depend on someone else's financial contribution to the household, this places you in a precarious position. And if you are in a precarious position within your relationship, it becomes far more difficult should you decide to exit, because you ARE tied to the role of being a volunteer; you have not laid the foundation of being self-sustaining.

Having boundaries and standards will provide you with the strength and courage you will need if you decide to leave a failing or unhappy relationship. What you are in effect doing while setting boundaries and having standards and demanding respect, is embarking on a new foundation of acquired skills that will assist you going forward. Strength is having the ability to walk away from a failing or unhappy relationship that is not going anywhere. If you are a weak-minded individual, you will never find the courage to walk away, the courage to let it go because you know in your heart of hearts it's not going to amount to anything positive. You can't *hold on and let go* – at the same time.

Having strength will make you rebound quicker. It will also allow you to put things in their true perspective. If you are without principles you will continue to constantly make one bad decision right after the other, and thereby ultimately prolong the inevitable – closure.

Standards, boundaries and strength are jewels that NONE of us are born with. These attributes are acquired throughout our life's journeys. They are part of our growth and development process. When we are born, we don't come with a set of instructions to help us navigate through life's journey. It's not that easy. You have to condition yourself by putting the lessons you learn in life into proper perspective. This is supposed to be part of your growth and development cycle as you age. This is how you grow and increase your intellect. If you don't allow yourself to learn from bad as well as good experiences, you will remain stagnant.

The process of learning from past mistakes will enable you to reposition yourself and also to make better decisions going forward. You'll be better equipped to make more informed decisions by utilizing what you have learned from past experiences. It's as simple as that. If you take a test and you choose "A" and then find out that "B" was the right answer, if you take that test again, you shouldn't/wouldn't pick "A" as the answer again, RIGHT? Yeah, I know, you see, but some of us will pick "A" as the answer time and time again. So by doing this, in effect means that they have learned NOTHING. Allowing yourself to constantly keep making the same mistake over and over again is how you become a VOLUNTEER. By making the same mistake let's say once or maybe even twice, you can claim to be a victim. Anything more than that, you're a volunteer.

<u>The Heart</u>
The heart as we all know is a key organ. The role it plays with respect to the body is very significant. However, we also use the word "heart" when describing our emotions. The heart when we use it in this sense controls and dictates the feelings that we encounter when something significant happens in our lives – when we experience love, hate, friendship, happiness, sadness, loneliness, just to name a few. Many of us have visited Heartbreak City more times that we care to remember. The feeling of having experienced a broken heart in a relationship can be described in many different ways. In some instances you may feel that you can't describe in it words. But you know what? You *can* describe it in words.

A broken heart is a wound that can be healed only with time. The wound could remain open and vulnerable for quite a long time. It's a feeling of emptiness. It's a feeling of disappointment. It's a feeling of betrayal. It's an empty feeling that's very hard to wrap your head around. It's very hard to find a place to park it without having to worry about it consuming you to the point where it takes control over your life in a negative way.

Allowing the emotion of love to consume one is the main reason many people stay in failing or unhappy relationships. They don't know how to navigate around the feelings that have led them to Heartbreak City. They also have not learned how to process the feelings of being heartbroken.

This is why they will continue to allow themselves to volunteer and accept the continuous bad behavior of their significant other. Perhaps they fear being alone. Perhaps they fear the experience of feeling the emotion of emptiness. That's why even though the bad times may outweigh the good- they will stay in the relationship. This is why entertaining the thought of trading a failing or unhappy relationship for emptiness becomes a difficult decision to make. This is why there is a tremendous need to not only let your heart be your guide, but the thoughts in your head as well.

When you are in a relationship, experiencing the emotion of love is a wonderful feeling. The person you have this love for sometimes can't be described in words. The way you describe and express the love you have for your significant other is for the most part through the things you do for them. I mean of course you can on occasion say "I love you" to your significant other, but it is your actions that speak volumes about you feeling of love. You can compare the emotion of love with all the other emotions that we experience from time to time: anger, lust, disappointment, sadness, happiness, etc. Each emotion is for the most part *controlled* in some form or fashion. If you're angry about a situation, eventually you process that anger and move forward. If you look at someone with lust eventually the emotion of lust passes and you move forward.

If something happens where you become disappointed, you process the disappointment and move forward. If a close relative/friend passes away, you process the loss and move forward. If something makes you happy, you process the happiness and move forward. So why, if you experience the emotion of heartache from a failed relationship, is it so difficult to process the heartache and move forward? Some of us continue for long periods of time and FAIL in our attempt to process that emotion of love in a failed relationship. Why is that? What happens is that some of us DON'T process it using the HEART in conjunction with the thoughts of the BRAIN about the relationship. This is what makes some of us continue to play the volunteer role longer than we should.

What a lot of us get stuck on is the time we have invested in the relationship. A lot of us also get stuck on the children who were conceived in the relationship. A lot of us also get stuck on wondering how we can survive without that person in our lives. And these are just to name a few.

Well, let me tell you this: #1 The time you have invested in the relationship will NEVER change. It certainly won't get any shorter. If anything, if you stay in that failing or unhappy relationship, the time invested will get longer, which, in effect, only means that you've volunteered much longer than you should have. #2 Any children who were conceived in the relationship will still BE THERE when the relationship is over. #3 Continuing- to prolong the inevitable, worrying about whether you'll be able to survive without that person in your life, only means that you have NO survival skills. No survival skills - equals no boundaries, standards, or principles.

You see, all our organs are connected to each other in some form or fashion. Sometimes those organs work in unison so that they yield the right results to keep us on a stable footing. All the organs are interconnected somehow. If you are in a failing or unhappy relationship and are contemplating getting out, you must use your brain (thought processes), in conjunction with your heart, in order to make the right decision. If you attempt to decide on leaving the failing or unhappy relationship with ONLY the emotions of your heart, you'll remain there for a long time to come. Using your head (the brain) in conjunction with the emotions you feel in your heart, will put things in a better perspective.

Working these organs in unison enables you to decide whether you are going to sink or swim. It won't be an easy decision by any stretch of the imagination. However, when you make the decision to exit out of your failing or unhappy relationship, in all probability, it'll be the right decision that will ultimately give you peace of mind.

If you are in a relationship where there is no peace of mind, you truly should NOT be there. And if there is only one person in the relationship trying to make it work, that in itself is a huge problem.

Some relationships are very hard to maintain. However, you should know that maintaining a positive relationship can be achieved without a doubt. Don't ever let anyone tell you that a successful relationship can't be accomplished. Now, if you are seeking a fairytale relationship, let me be the first to tell you that those types of relationships for the most part only exist in fairytale books.

So, if you make the decision to stay in a failing or unhappy relationship, know that you are not a VICTIM, you are a VOLUNTEER. You can't *hold on* and *let go* at the same time. Some of us try to hold on by using our children as pawns in a failing relationship. Some of use excuse after excuse in preventing the baby's daddy from seeing his son or his daughter. That is one of the worst mistakes some of us make.

If you know in you heart of hearts that your relationship is over, let your child's father see his son or daughter, especially if he wants to. And especially if you know he will do so responsibly. Don't place unrealistic conditions on his effort to see his child. Don't get upset with him when you find out that he has moved on with someone else. Don't be upset with him if he brings his new girl with him to pick up little Johnny or little Audrey. It's not like she's coming inside your apartment/house, and you have to make her breakfast...LMAO... Don't be upset with him if he is not contributing monetarily toward the child as you think he should be. Don't be upset with him if, when he drops off his child, and he doesn't stay around a bit longer so that he can kick it with you. Don't say bad things about him around your son or daughter. Doing these types things show that you're still trying to hold on.

You should be happy if he wants to spend time with his child, and give him kudos for wanting to do so. You should be grateful that he wants to continue to play the father role in the life of the child you and he made together. Don't set bogus preconditions for allowing him to see his child. Now all of a sudden he is the worst person in the world because he is no longer in your life. At one point in time he was the best thing that ever happened to you. He had to be. You chose to have a baby with him. I think you get the point.

Your primary focus with respect to allowing your child's father to see children is that #1 He comes to pick the child up at the prescribed time. #2 He drops the child off at the agreed time. # 3 He delivers what he says he is going to deliver. Don't concern yourself about the nuances. This is where you get yourself into trouble. If you know that your child's father is a responsible individual, why would you not want him to spend time helping to raise the children alongside you? Children should have BOTH parents in their lives even if the parents are no longer a couple. Think about the break you will get. Keep it simple and remember: it's not about you, it's about the child.

Love
Love is a wonderful feeling to have for someone or something. Through life's travels, everyone will experience the emotion of love in a relationship. True love in a relationship with a significant other, will make you surrender your heart to the extent that no other person or thing can penetrate that love you have for your significant other. There will be nothing that you will allow to come between the emotions of love you have in your relationship. You will not allow anything or anyone to disrupt that flow.

Oftentimes, for some of us the feeling of love is indescribable. The emotion of true love will make you want to protect that person unconditionally, even if it means sacrificing your life on earth to do so. True love could also make you want to live with that person for the rest of your life. It's a wonderful feeling when is not misguided.

Men who cheat
I bet a great deal many of you are still trying to figure out why men cheat. Well, let me tell you what I think the REAL reason is. It has more to do about the man than it has to do about you. It has nothing to do with how you look, how you perform in the bedroom, how you manage the household, or how you stroke his ego. They cheat because they don't have the necessary *maturity and intellect* to remain faithful in their relationship. You see, men who exhibit the behavior of a cheater can be best described in one word. Or maybe two words, "intellectually immature." They don't have the intellectual maturity that restrains them from seeking pleasure of any kind, outside their relationship. There are many individuals who, while in a committed relationship LUST at someone else. And when you lust at someone else while in a committed relationship you do so while imagining all the things you would like to do to that person. Or better yet, you can imagine all the things that the person can do to you. The KEY is to NOT put that emotion of LUST into action. Men inherently look at other women. That's simply the nature of the beast. Now if he looks at the other woman while he is with you, he should do so through his peripheral vision. This way, he does not risk disrespecting you or the relationship.

Only intellectually immature men cheat on the woman that they are in a committed relationship with. If you are in a relationship with someone and you are unhappy, or if that person is not turning you on anymore, or if the thrill is GONE, you should end the relationship before you attempt to move on. Trying to have the best of both worlds, means that you are trying to hold and let go to, AT THE SAME TIME. The saying "once a *cheater always a cheater*" isn't necessarily so. That statement is contingent upon the degree of maturity acquired, if any, by that man after having previously been known as a cheater. An example of a man who is intellectually immature is one who knows he's prone to dealing with a multitude of woman. And then let's say he decides to get married, and while he's married, he continues to deal with a multitude of woman. The behavior he is exhibiting is nothing more than intellectual immaturity. Simple as that! You see men who treat intimacy casually, typically treat women the very same way.

Need vs. want
When it comes to independent women, a lot of us take heat for being self-sustaining. It's been said that a man has to feel *needed* in the relationship that he is in. So when it comes to independent women, since we supposedly don't need a man to pay our bills, because we pay them ourselves; and since we don't need a man to help us buy a house, because we already own a house; and since we don't

need to ask a man to borrow his car, because we already have our own car; because of this, a man then feels that you don't NEED him. Men who view independent women as not NEEDING a man should really view that woman like this in a much more positive way. A man should look at a woman's independence whereby he should have the ultimate comfort in knowing that she is with him because she WANTS to be with him. Don't you think it would be much more comforting to know that your desire for someone should be more of a WANT, than that of a NEED? UMMM.. In short, don't allow a man to fault you for what you have acquired through your journey in life.

<u>Men of a certain age</u>
If you are dealing with a man who is let's say 50+ years old and he is still living at home with his mother, OMG run for dear life. If he's not living with his mother because he is providing her with medical care, and he has been there for an extended period of time – this speaks volumes...careful now. In short, if a man is 50+ years of age and you see that he has not established a decent foundation for himself at this point in time, there is NO point in you indulging with him, unless you plan on carrying him, as dead weight. You must watch for the signs while in the dating arena because they tell you the entire story. And that story, if you are paying attention will reveal to you # 1 Where he is **AT** #2 Where he has **BEEN** #3 Where he is **GOING**. PAY ATTENTION!!!! LOL

Friendships/relationships
Lots of people define friendships or relationships in many different ways. One way to describe them is an affirmation, an alliance or bond between individuals. Sometimes, just because someone may refer to you as being their friend doesn't necessarily mean that you should expect them to play an integral role in your life forever. In life, people cross paths with each other for many different reasons. Maybe that person is only meant to be in your life for a certain period of time. And when that time expires, that relationship or friendship can take on an entirely different meaning.

Being realistic, all relationships or friendships are NOT meant to last forever. Oftentimes, in life, people that you cross paths with, you do so solely for the purpose of learning experiences. They are only there for the purpose of a teaching moment. You will find that oftentimes we are quick to sever ties with people who we should really hold on to. And then on the other hand, we are NOT quick enough in severing ties with people who we should LET GO OF!

Emptiness/loneliness
These two words are tough in that they are emotions that most people would hate to have to experience. And I couldn't agree with them more. However, when you are feeling as such, you must look at the broad spectrum while performing your analysis. And part of that analysis should be

concentrated not only on what you think you DON'T have, but also on what it is that you DO have.

You might be experiencing the feeling of being EMPTY in one regard, but what about the feeling of being FULL in another? You have to look for some sense of balance. And that balance doesn't always have to be in the form of companionship. Concentrate on both aspects of Full/Empty instead of just one, i.e. unison, which I spoke about in an earlier chapter. There is no one person in the world who can claim that their every need/want is being fulfilled.

Loneliness is also a feeling relative to emptiness. Here again, you have to look at the broad spectrum while performing your analysis. You may feel lonely because you don't have a significant other. However, being ALONE (without companionship) doesn't necessarily constitute loneliness. There are other things you can indulge yourself in that can help fill the empty void.

There are a great deal many people who are in relationships, living with their significant other every single day and they are still experiencing the feeling of emptiness/loneliness. In short, being a little THIRSTY, to some people, is a far better place to be in, by comparison. Hmmm! Y'ALL know what I'm talking about when I say a little THIRSTY – right? LMAO

Please – they have a bunch of THIRST QUENCHERS out here nowadays! LMAO...

Chapter 9 – Final chapter

Life's experiences with failed attempts at a meaningful relationship

This is the closing chapter of my book. This isn't a long book in terms of pages, but it's long on substance. However, after reading this, you should be in a better place mentally in the event that you are contemplating moving forward from a failing or unhappy relationship and leaving behind the volunteer role that you could be playing.

If you elect to remain in a failing or unhappy relationship, make no mistake, you won't be able to detect every lie, you won't be able to withstand every game, you won't be able to see certain circumstances from miles away, but what you WILL and should be able to accomplish, if you take note, is navigating your way around the nonsense, with minimal damage to your integrity. What you WILL also know how to do is spot when the direction of the WIND is changing in your relationship. And when you spot that wind change, you WILL know how and WHEN to adjust your SAILS. Adjusting your SAILS will be nothing more than pulling the ACTIVATION button on your boundaries so that your safety mechanisms will release whatever blockage is required to prevent you from falling HARD.

Unfortunately, many people fall several times back to back after having been in one or more bad relationships. The take away is what you do when YOU GET UP. Do you set yourself up to become a volunteer time and time again, OR do you learn from past mistakes? And learning from past mistakes, do you try to incorporate your boundaries and standards in potential relationships going forward?

Oftentimes, you will encounter many friends and/or family members who will tell you that your boundaries and standards are unrealistic. Don't second guess yourself. As long as you know in you heart of hearts that what you are seeking in a relationship does NOT border on being absurd, then you are exactly where you need to be.

So I pose this question to you: ARE YOU A VICTIM OR A VOLUNTEER?

You must learn how to envision what the possible outcome would be if you elect to get into a relationship with someone who would NOT complement what you have already established in your life. The person you decide to become involved with must possess the tools needed to make the relationship healthy. If he doesn't possess these, then you should be able to make an informed decision to keep it moving. If you become involved with someone who does not have the tools required to maintain a healthy relationship, know that ultimately the relationship will be doomed.

So proceed with caution, and don't allow yourself to become a victim for too long. And more importantly, don't become a *volunteer* of misery, pain and stress.

ARE YOU A VICTIM OR A VOLUNTEER?

IF YOU ARE a victim in a failing or unhappy relationship, START PREPARING YOUR EXIT STRATEGY.

A victim in a relationship
A victim in a relationship is someone who has made a commitment after having been wooed and has been masterfully tricked into thinking that the man she has just committed to is everything that she deludedly thinks he is. His masterful skills during his courtship convinced you that he was the one you had been looking for all this time. He has, however, only let you see the *representative* side of him. He has skillfully represented himself to be this smooth, charming, alluring man who has been on a mission to find that perfect woman who will succumb to every wicked intention that he has outlined only to himself. He has skillfully set his goal around conditioning you to be everything that he wants you to be. And the role he ultimately wants you to play is that of a victim or a volunteer.

However, once you have unmasked his intentions, you don't stick around for his kill. You set your wheels in motion and prepare for your dismount out of his life, because you know that his intentions for you are not what you are looking for. It is at this point in time that you realize that you were a victim of his masterful skills. So you bounce!

A volunteer in a relationship
A volunteer, on the other hand, will allow a man to come through back door during the courtship period. And when I say "back door" I mean that you possibly already knew that he was in some sort of relationship. The "back door" also means that you knew he had issues. The "back door" means that his behavior was indicative of that of a loser. The "back door" means that you know he has baby momma drama. Once he has entered through the back door, and you continue seeking a relationship with him, you can't expect anything other than bad behavior.

A month has passed by, and no doubt his bad behavior continues, and before you know it, a year has passed by with his continued bad behavior. And now it has been two years that has gone by and still he has continued his bad behavior. So now you have invested all this time with him; so you're looking for results that you were NEVER going to get in the first place, because you pretended that the bad behavior did not exist. You deluded yourself to the point where you were convinced that you would be able to change him.

By now you've accepted the bad behavior for so long that you begin to make excuses for his bad behavior.

You have begun to accept his bad behavior as the norm. And it is indeed the norm, because you have allowed him to come through the back door. He's not about to change anything to please you. You accepted his bad behavior from the beginning, so he now feels that he is not obligated to change anything to make the relationship work. In short, since you have allowed him to come through the back, it will now become self-defeating for you to expect him to be *up front* with you about why he is exhibiting this type of behavior. He has accomplished his goal. His goal was to put you exactly where he wanted you.

You have compromised your integrity to the point where he now knows he has total control of your emotions. He has positioned himself in your life, to the point where you will, for the most part, succumb to his every command. Sure, you'll put up a fuss about some of his bad behavior, but once you continue to sleep with him knowing what you know, you're exactly where he wants you to be.

Even though you have confronted him about his bad behavior, he won't change it, because you are still sleeping with him. Why you would even expect him to change? All this makes you a volunteer. A volunteer remains in a failing or unhappy relationship after knowing that she is being played. A volunteer remains in a relationship after having evidence of infidelity. A volunteer remains in a relationship after she knows that the man's primary interest in her is sexual. A volunteer remains in a relationship thinking that the situation will change after she has confronted him about it time and time again.

A volunteer is someone who knows that her significant other fathered a child outside of their relationship and yet still remains in that relationship. A volunteer is someone who constantly allows herself to be physically or mentally abused for an extended period of time and yet chooses to stay in that failing or unhappy relationship. In spite of all of the above mentioned, don't consider yourself doomed. Just because you might NOT think you have any integrity left, does NOT mean you can't acquire any.

<u>The take away from this book is the following</u>
1) If you have been in a failing or unhappy relationship for an extended period of time, you should begin to prepare yourself for exiting that failing or unhappy relationship.

2) If you don't have any boundaries with respect to your relationship, you must find some and incorporate them into your daily life.

3) Don't feel that you need to have a man in your life in order to validate your womanhood.

4) Don't continuously accept the bad behavior of your significant other.

5) Demand that your significant other respect the relationship.

6) Don't try to *hold on and let go* to at the same time if you are trying to get out of a failing or unhappy relationship.

7) Be firm when you make your decision to exit from your failing or unhappy relationship.

8) Never love too deeply to the point where you accept bad behavior from your significant other for an extended period of time.

9) Equip yourself with the necessary tools that will assist you when you have decided to exit a failing or unhappy relationship.

10) Know that the emotion of love doesn't mean that you should allow yourself to be held captive.

11) Know that you can still be in love with your significant other even if you have made the decision to exit out of the relationship.

12) Know that being alone and uncommitted is not the worst possible place you can be.

13) Know that there is somebody else out there who will love you and respect you for who you are.

14) Know that you DO have the capability of surviving in the world without being attached to someone who brings you constant emotional turmoil.

15) Learn how to master the skill of being able to close the door on a failing or unhappy relationship without looking back.

16) Learn how to say NO to that revolving door of volunteering.

17) If you are in a failing or unhappy relationship and you want out of that failing or unhappy relationship, just convince yourself with every fiber of your being that this is not where you should be, and start executing the necessary actions to exit out of that failing or unhappy relationship.

18) Don't put men who exhibit bad behavior on pedestals and allow them to THINK that they are entitled to behave in this manner.

19) Be sure that your significant other acknowledges that your feelings are just as IMPORTANT as his.

20) Keep copious notes when you make your compatibility check list for potential mates, going forward

21) Don't allow anyone to continuously beat down your spirit.

22) Remember without BOUNDARIES, STANDARDS, and PRINCIPLES, when it comes to navigating yourself out of bad-behavior situations within your relationship, you will be forced to MAKE IT UP AS YOU GO ALONG

23) CLOSE THE BACK DOOR!!!!!!!!!!!!!!!!!!!

Don't be afraid of the tough interior that you will establish by putting forward and keeping in place your newly found boundaries, standards, and principles. These are simply a few tools that will prevent you from endlessly accepting the role of a VOLUNTEER.

Good luck! /Good skill! /GOD BLESS!

Epilogue

The purpose of my deciding to write this book was not to tear women down or to make them feel bad about themselves. The objective was to attempt to empower women with the tools they MUST have in order to find some degree of happiness within their relationship. At the age of 53, I've seen so many women who are in places within their relationship that they do not know how to escape from. And as a result, they continue to make one bad decision right after the other, not learning anything from their past mistakes. So this is why I felt compelled to share the knowledge and opinions that I have with others. And there you have it! I'm outta here.

PEACE OUT…….

Made in the USA
Charleston, SC
24 September 2011